At Home in Exile

The Journey Towards a New Paradigm

Peter McDowell

First Published in 2012

Contemporary Christianity

Belfast

www.contemporarychristianity.net

© Peter McDowell

Printed by Asdon Group

Cover design by Åsa McDowell

ISBN   978-1-87432-402-7

CONTEMPORARY
CHRISTIANITY
BIBLICAL FAITH FOR
A CHANGING WORLD

Contents

Jeremiah's Field

Weep, weep not for me,
but weep for yourselves
for the day has ended.
Weep not for me
for the night must come
before the morning.
This is the time, the time
for seeking the Lord,
This is the time, the time
for weeping before Him.
Now is the time,
the time for returning.
Set up the waymarks!
turn your hearts
towards the highway.
Turn again,
turn again,
O virgin Israel.
Return to the Lord.

Meditation for Day 11
Celtic Daily Prayer[1]

---

1 Northumbria Community and Northumbria Community Staff, *Celtic Daily Prayer* (London: Harper Collins, 2005), p 56.

Preface

Uncomfortable as it is we have to face facts; the Church in Britain is declining. Even in Northern Ireland, where the influence of Christendom still holds some influence, resorting to denial or some kind of plea-bargaining will not change the prognosis of a diminishing church. Thriving churches and renewal movements have not stemmed the tide of decline. Praying fervently, preaching passionately and singing triumphalist songs and hymns, that hold as much promise for the future as the Titanic did on its maiden voyage, aren't reversing the facts that in Western consumer society the drift is away from God and his ways, not toward them.

Propagating a false sense of hope and belief that revival is just around the corner is to behave like Jeremiah's contemporaries who, "healed the hurt of my people slightly saying, 'Peace, peace' when there is no peace." To do so would not only be foolish but it would blind us to what God is seeking to do through taking his people into exile. The last thing we need is people trying to soothe us with a wrong diagnosis. What we need, are people who will help us to see the reality of what is happening. People who, motivated by faith, not driven by fear, can lead us with courage and compassion on a journey into the new things that God is seeking to do among us. In Peter we have such a person. Through his writings he confronts us with issues that we may wish to avoid. He encourages us to discover again the language of exile which helps our understanding and interpreting of what is emerging within the church and wider society. He informs our awareness of the context, challenges and opportunities that we face as the people of God living through inevitable change.

Surveying the Scriptures we are reminded how God uses periods of exile to both call us back to himself and his ways but also to discover, in the words of Walter Brueggemann, a new way to be human in the world.

The experience of change presents us with many challenges and opportunities. Change evokes feelings of insecurity and uncertainty which in turn calls forth a response of faith, not fear.

Peter's book is an invaluable companion for the people of God being taken into exile. Its challenging insights, observations and analysis are complemented by encouragement and hope to journey into an unknown future with a known God and to be at home in exile.

Roy Searle

Leader, Northumbria Community
August 2012

Introduction: Choosing the Right Metaphor

The origins of this essay lie in a conversation at a retreat for church leaders that I attended in 2010. The retreat was being led by Roy Searle, a founder-member of the Northumbria Community. One evening Roy was sharing the story of the community and told how he had been asked to speak at a certain church in England. About twenty years later he was invited to speak again, and returning to the church he found that they were still praying for revival and singing the same revival songs. He felt that he had to tell them that revival had not come, and that it probably was not coming. Relating the story to us he reflected that the most appropriate metaphor for the church today was that of exile. His words struck a chord within me, both personally and as I seek to understand my role as minister of a congregation in this place and time. This essay is written as an exploration of this metaphor for the church in general, but more particularly as a means of reflecting on my own ministry.

The Bible is the story of God's people and his dealings with them. It records various stages in their life, from their call and formation in the stories of Moses and the Exodus, through the more settled temple period, to the trauma of the exile and finally the expansion of the book of Acts. At each stage of the biblical story God's people were organised in a particular way and worshipped in particular ways. Thus, the community of faith during the time of the judges was very different from that during the monarchy, which was in turn very different from the period in which Jesus ministered.

At different times, and in its varying contexts, the church has found that different parts of the scriptural story resonates with it more than others. The church is naturally drawn to that stage of the life of God's people in scripture which bears most similarity to its context. The resulting emphasis on this part of scripture then influences the understanding of what church is, what it does and how it relates to the world around it. While we must always seek to draw our understanding of the church from all parts of scripture, it is natural that we are drawn to that part of scripture which most closely matches our own context, and that this becomes the primary metaphor by which we understand the church. At a time of societal change it is perhaps inevitable that the predominant biblical metaphor underlying our understanding of church will also change. At such a time it is vital that the appropriate Biblical metaphor is selected to replace it, for this metaphor will inform our practice and methods, as well as our expectations.

One significant metaphor from the Old Testament which has been influential is that of the temple period. This was the period when Israel was established in its own land, with its own independent political structure and a national religion centred on the temple. Walter Brueggeman has argued that this model was the natural metaphor for the church during the era of Christendom, since it fits easily in a context of an established church closely linked with the surrounding culture.[2] He lists four features of the temple period. First, there were visible and stable religious structures, with a legitimated leadership. Second, the political and religious structures were,

---

2   Walter Brueggemann and Patrick D Miller, *A Social Reading of the Old Testament - Prophetic Approaches to Israel's Communal Life* (Minneapolis: Fortress Press, 1994), p 263–275.

at least publicly, committed to the same theological view of the world, so much so that the temple functioned pretty much as the 'royal chapel'. Third, within this system an intelligentsia arose which was influential in ensuring that the established religion encouraged the stabilisation of power and knowledge. Fourth, it was the sharing by the religious and civil leadership of the presuppositions at the heart of the religion that allowed for the ministry of the prophets. As Brueggemann puts it, 'The voice of passion is viable only in a social circumstance where established powers are in principle committed to the same conversation.'[3]

It is clear that each of these features of the temple period is applicable to the church in the period of Christendom. One key feature of the temple period, mirrored in the period of Christendom, is that the civic leadership and the religious structure were committed to the same basic world view. In the 1950's Lesslie Newbigin, then working as a missionary in India, reflected on the different social contexts of the church in India and the West at the time. He saw that within Christendom the church was able to 'take it for granted that by far the greater part of the secular affairs of their members are conducted without any direct relationship to the Church.'[4] In areas of education, medicine, politics, economics etc. church members looked for guidance, not to the church, but to acknowledged experts in each sphere. The church could confine itself simply to the 'religious' concerns of its members because secular society was still 'so much shaped by its origin

---

3   Ibid., p 265–6.
4   Lesslie Newbigin, *The Household of God* (London: SCM Press, 1951), p 14.

in a single Christian conception and practice of life.'[5] In India the church had to be actively engaged in many more areas of the lives of its members, precisely because it did not share the same worldview as the surrounding society. Already, in the 1950's Newbigin recognised that the relationship between the western church and secular society was changing, which had implications for the assumption that the church could simply concentrate on the religious life of its members. It is also interesting to note that Brueggemann states that the temple religion acted as a chaplain to the the society, which is exactly how the church in Christendom saw its role, according to Newbigin.

Brueggemann also sounds a warning about the temple metaphor in relationship to the church. It is often assumed that the temple period marked the high-point of the life of God's people in the Old Testament; that this is the purest metaphor for the church before we reach the book of Acts. However, even during this period it is clear that there was political accommodation, complacency and syncretism with the religions of the neighbouring nations. We shall follow this point up later.

The temple metaphor was a natural one for the church in Christendom, but it is now widely accepted that the Christendom era is over. The church no longer has a privileged or accepted place in society. The shared conceptions about life and practice between the church and society have gone. The church is a minority in a world which does not share its beliefs or values, and which is often antagonistic. The

---

5   Ibid.

church is struggling to find its place in this new society and a new metaphor for understanding the church is needed.

Perhaps the most natural place to turn is to the early church. This period in the life of God's people has been considered normative for the church through all ages. The giving of the Holy Spirit at Pentecost marked a definitive new stage in the life of God's people. It was the fulfilment of God's promises to his people after the crucial work of Christ, described as a mystery which had been long hidden, but now was revealed. It marked the beginning of the post-Pentecost period in which the church still exists. It is natural, therefore, that the models and forms of the early church have inspired and challenged the church since then.

Another reason that the the early church metaphor appeals in the post-Christendom context is that there are numerous similarities between the two contexts. The early church was a small minority in the Roman Empire. It was a church on the margins and had no formal link to the state. It had no privileges, and its beliefs and values often clashed with those of the society around it, so that it often struggled to get its voice heard. It also existed in the midst of vibrant, attractive and exotic religious competition, and in an atmosphere of religious pluralism. These similarities make it a tempting metaphor to turn to as the church comes to terms with its new and evolving relationship with post-Christendom society.

However, the similarities between the current context and the early church's context should not blind us to the differences that also exist. The early church, as described in the New Testament, was a church in the full flush of new life. It grew spontaneously and rapidly in many directions. There is evidence of a missionary strategy in the life of Paul,[6] but the plans of church leaders often had to be adapted due to circumstances. Yet, even when things that appeared on the surface to be problems occurred, they invariably led to further missionary success. When a new congregation was established it was a new entity formed by the conversion of people from various religious backgrounds. The church was growing and had an incredible confidence, even in the face of persecution. It showed creativity and courageous thinking as it developed its life and traditions, for even though it had grown out of the Jewish tradition, and drew from its sources, it did not have a tradition of its own to draw on. The leaders of congregations were often very new Christians with little knowledge or training, and new believers had to struggle to work out the implications of their new faith in the context of the society in which they had grown up. Despite all of these problems and the disputes that arose from them there was an atmosphere of commitment, confidence and expectation.

The metaphor of the early church fits some situations in the modern world very well. The church in Nepal, for example, was born in the 1950's into a predominantly hostile Hindu environment. It has faced similar problems to the early church, in that it has very few trained leaders and its members have had to figure out what shape the church in Nepal should take. They have struggled with persecution and the task of forging a place in society. There have been problems of division and theological disagreements. In spite of all this the church has grown to over a million people within fifty years. The growth has come both through planned outreach activities and

6 See Roland Allen, *Missionary Methods - St Paul's or Ours?* (Grand Rapids, Michigan: Eerdmans, 1968).

powerful workings of the Spirit. The atmosphere in the Nepali church is one of commitment, confidence and expectation.

The same cannot be said when we turn to the church in Britain. Here the church has a long history during which the temple metaphor was appropriate, but which is now ending. The church has a long tradition and has been used to holding a privileged place in society, but is aware that this is changing rapidly. The numbers attending church are declining and, despite occasional success stories, the church is struggling to find ways to communicate the gospel in a meaningful way to those outside. There is an overall sense of decline and loss of confidence.

The early church metaphor is attractive because it is positive and hopeful. It points to success and increasing influence, which in difficult times are tempting to aspire to. We may even feel that it would be unfaithful and unbelieving not to hold to this hope. However, before jumping to adopt this as our predominant metaphor for understanding church in our context we must examine all the alternatives. We must ask if there is a more appropriate metaphor that more accurately fits the current context, that will provide the right set of expectations and thus be a helpful basis on which to build our working model of the church.

Brueggemann suggests that the period of the exile has much to offer the church in North America as it faces the end of a period in which the temple model predominated. It is perhaps even more applicable as a metaphor for the church in Britain. The exile period shares many similarities with the early church period. It was a period where God's people were marginalised and had no formal access to state power. They also had to discern what it meant to live faithfully in a pluralist society, with many other competing, and apparently more successful, religions. The key difference, however, is that whereas the early church was bursting into its society with the full confidence of new life and was growing rapidly, the people of the exile were dealing with the loss of established structures and of influence, along with theological questions and doubts, combined with a crisis of confidence. The haunting question of God's people entering and living in exile was 'How do we sing the Lord's song in a strange land?' It is a question that churches in Britain are asking as society changes around them, as many of the certainties they took for granted crumble to dust and the old ways of being the church become impossible to maintain. It is the asking of this question, along with the underlying feelings of confusion and loss, that make the exile an appropriate metaphor for the church at this time.

While there are similarities between the current situation of the church and the period of the exile, there are also important differences. In the exile the people were physically removed from their land to live in nations which had no background of faith in Yahweh, or knowledge of him. The 'exile' faced by the church in Britain does not involve a geographical shift. For the churches in Britain it is not that they have been deported to a strange empire, but that a strange 'empire' is developing around it and gaining ever more influence so that the church no longer feels at home. Unlike the empires of the original exile this empire is not ignorant of the church's faith. In fact it has been profoundly influenced by it, even if it has forgotten, or chooses to ignore its debt. Yet, this modern empire is similar to the ancient ones in that it basically sees the church and its faith as irrelevant and insignificant. This, in fact, mirrors the situation for the people who returned from exile to live in Israel. In spite of their high expectations things did not return to the way they had been before. The construction of the new temple was greeted with both joy and mourning. Joy from the younger people who thought they would never see the day, and tears from the older people who could remember the glory of the first temple. The people never regained full political control of their land and were thus forced to live with permanent compromise between their faith and their political life. Different groups posited different strategies for living in this new context and there were disagreements among them over the appropriate way to live as the people of God. As N.T. Wright puts it, even after their return the people felt as if the experience of exile was continuing.[7] They had to learn to be at home in exile.

The exilic and post-exilic periods may not be as attractive a metaphor for the church as the early church period. It was not a period of great numerical growth, but of perceived loss. God's people resisted the idea that exile might be coming because it was so inconceivable to their understanding of God and themselves as his people. It was a time of crisis when their very existence as a people appeared to be in the balance. It was also a time of theological crisis as they sought to understand what had happened and how they were to live faithfully in an environment they had not been prepared for. But it was ultimately an intensely formative period and one in which God was active. It was the exile experience that led to the development of synagogue worship, which was an entirely new way of structuring the life and worship of God's people.

---

7   N. T Wright, *The New Testament and the People of God* (Fortress Press, 1996), p 269.

It led to a focus on the scriptures, to a reconsideration of the tradition and to new insights that ultimately paved the way for the coming of Christ. There were also surprising and noticeable times of mission, in spite of the weakness and marginalisation of the people.

This essay is written in the belief that the metaphor of exile is the most appropriate metaphor for the church in Britain at this time. The decline in church membership and its loss of influence in a changing society are not a passing trend but a new phase of life that the church must come to terms with. Change is being, and will be, forced on the church in various ways. This change will mean that the old ways of organising and structuring church will no longer be effective or possible. The changes will lead to various experiments in areas of church life. There will be competing views among Christians about how to live a faithful life in a new social context which the past has not prepared us for. There will be church closures and fewer full-time trained church leaders. The loss of influence and closures of churches will require theological answers to the questions of where God is in the process and about the very nature of the church itself.

It has been shown that individuals and organisations go through similar processes when dealing with change. In the 1980s Elizabeth Kubler Ross observed that people facing bereavement moved through various stages of grief. Her work has been developed to help understand how individuals and organisations react to change and is often represented by the change curve.[8]

---

8   This version taken from University of Exeter, 'The Change Curve', June 27, 2011, http://www.exeter.ac.uk/media/universityofexeter/humanreso

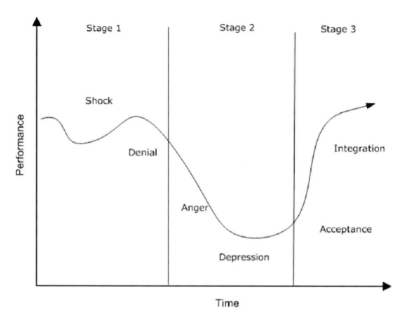

Figure 1: The Change Curve

The curve shows three stages: shock and denial, anger and depression and acceptance and integration. The remainder of this essay will use these three stages as a structure to explore the metaphor of exile in relation to the contemporary experience of the church in Britain. It will also explore the associated pastoral responsibilities noted by Brueggemann at each stage[9]. The period of shock and denial relates to the period immediately before the exile when Israel was being warned of what was to come, but could not accept it. The appropriate pastoral task at this stage is to help people enter exile. The period of anger and depression accurately describes

urces/documents/learningdevelopment/the_change_curve.pdf.
9   Walter Brueggemann, *Hopeful Imagination: Prophetic Voices in Exile* (Philadelphia: Fortress Press, 1986), 1.

the experience of the people in exile when they had just been deported and were asking 'how do we sing the Lord's song in a strange land?' The associated pastoral task is to help people be in exile. The stage of acceptance and integration describes the period in which the people adapted to their new context and began to develop the new expression of faith, community life and worship that would be the next paradigm for God's people. The pastoral task for this stage is to help the people depart from exile.

The paradigm that emerged out of the exile experience was the one into which Christ was born and was ultimately the foundation for the growth of the early church. Exile may be a profoundly traumatic and difficult experience from which there is no return to the way things were before. But, it may also, in God's plan, be the means of causing a new paradigm for the church to come into being.

Entering Exile: Shock and Denial

According to the change curve the first reaction to change is often shock and denial, and this is certainly the response Israel had to the prospect of exile. The exile did not come about suddenly, but was preceded by many years of internal and external political and social problems. Israel was very aware of the ebbs and flows of international politics at the time and its precarious position in the midst of it all. The problems and dangers were not disputed, it was the causes and solutions that were the subject of debate. Some prophets argued that through these events God was warning his people that change was necessary, otherwise God would bring the monarchy and temple worship to an end by exiling his people. Many simply could not accept this. They argued that God would not, perhaps even could not, do such a thing. They argued that God had chosen his people and had given them the land. The temple and its worship were ordained by him. It was therefore inconceivable that he would bring it to an end. For many people their faith in God was tied up with these issues. If there were to be no temple there would be no means by which to relate to God. If Israel were to be driven out of the land it would imply either that God had rejected his people, or that he was not as powerful as the gods of the other nations. It is all too easy for us reading with the benefit of hindsight to lose sight of the intense debate there was over how to interpret events and trends.

Similarly there is debate about how to interpret the current situation of the church in Britain and how we should respond. There is an awareness of a problem, even a crisis – the statistics of church decline speak for themselves. There is recognition that the church must respond, but the correct response to a problem requires a true understanding of the problem. We are faced with a society which is becoming post-Christian[10] and the church is in rapid decline. The question is how fundamental the changes in society are and how radical the effect on the church will be in the long term. We need to ask if the changes are reversible. Can we return to a Christian society? Can the church regain or retain its influence? Then we need to consider the implications for the church. Can the church continue to operate in the same way but with minor changes? Or will the church change dramatically, so that what emerges is almost unrecognisable from what we have now? We need to consider the meaning of the events and changes that are happening. Are they an indication of the apostasy of the western world? Are they an indication of the defeat, death or irrelevance of God in the modern world? Or could God actually be actively involved in the process? If so, what is he doing? These questions are very similar to those exercising the people in Jerusalem before the exile.

The intense debate prior to the exile is clearly presented in the book of Jeremiah. As we approach this book it is helpful to try to imagine the situation from the perspective of the people Jeremiah was addressing. It appears that most of the society, that is, the political class, the priests and the people, saw themselves as God's people and that this offered them some degree of protection. They saw the system of worship in the temple as being ordained by God and pleasing to him, and

---

10 I am aware that there is debate as to whether western society has ever been 'Christian', but it is undeniable that the Christian heritage had a profound effect in moulding that society and that the influence of that heritage is rapidly diminishing.

could therefore conceive of no other way of worship and relating to him. They considered that they were worshippers of Yahweh and reacted strongly to suggestions that they were not, saying "That's not true! I haven't worshipped the images of Baal."[11]   The religious system was closely tied to the political system, each legitimising the other. It was, therefore, hard to conceive of being a follower of Yahweh anywhere but in the land he had given to his people, with a political order that was based on Yahwist principles and worship centred around the temple. All of these assumptions led to the belief that God would have to step in to prevent the loss of these through defeat to foreign powers. If God did not step in to save his people there were two possible interpretations, either that he was not powerful enough[12] or that he had judged his people and abandoned them. Threats from external nations like Egypt and Babylon were therefore profoundly troubling and had to be resisted. Anyone who expressed a different opinion was liable to be thought of as having little faith or being a traitor against his God and his people. This explains Hananiah's 'revivalist' response to Jeremiah when he predicted a reversal of the first exile and the re-establishment of full temple worship.[13]

In contrast to this Jeremiah brought a radically different interpretation. According to Jeremiah the entire political and religious edifice was systematically corrupt. Although it claimed to be centred on Yahweh, it was, in fact, religiously

---

11 Jer 2:23 (NLT) c.f. 2:35. See also 8:8 where it is clear that they feel their system is built on Yahweh's word.
12 Jer 14:8-9.
13 Jer 28:1-11.

idolatrous and socially oppressive[14] and as such Yahweh would bring it to an end. He pointed out that the religious and political system had been diverted over time from a devotion to Yahweh to become a syncretistic system with Yahwist roots and veneer,[15] and with a powerful and coherent justifying theology and religious system which sustained it. Some of the negative response to Jeremiah's words stemmed from those who had vested interests which made them reluctant to face the possibility of losing their power. It also came from those who simply could not theologically conceive of any other way of worship than that which they saw as ordained by God. They were incapable of seeing the systemic corruption, because such corruption is almost always invisible to those who are part of the system. Those who were part of this system could concede that there were some areas in which the system was not ideal, but they could not conceive that the entire system might be hopelessly corrupted. Thus, they could not formulate adequate responses to the deep systemic problems, but could only "offer superficial treatments" and "give assurances of peace where there is no peace".[16] This blindness accounts for the bewilderment expressed at Jeremiah's accusations of idolatry, when looking from the outside it is obvious that Yahweh was being worshipped alongside other gods. People honestly believed that they were living and worshipping as Yahweh's people and could not see

---

14 See e.g. Jer 2:34, 5:26-31, 7:6 etc.

15 An indication of this is seen in Jer 2:8 where the priests continue their work but do not ask 'Where is the LORD'. See also Jer 8:8-9 where the people state "We are wise because we have the word of the LORD", while Jeremiah argues that they have handled the word falsely and in fact rejected it (Jer 8:8-9).

16 Jer 6:14 (NLT), c.f. 8:11.

the inconsistencies in the system of worship they had grown up with.

Trying to understand things from the perspective of those Jeremiah was addressing allows us to understand how they felt that God would intervene on their behalf to save their country and their temple. They were God's people, so he must intervene. The leaders and prophets would have seen it as their pastoral responsibility to say 'Peace, peace' and to point people to the temple as an assurance that God would act for them. The sad truth, however, was that they were blinded by a combination of wishful thinking, vested interests and the blindness of growing up within the system. This led them to completely misinterpret the situation. It also inevitably led to the wrong response to the problems they were facing, to actively resisting God and making the situation worse. In the face of the problems which threatened them they basically wanted things to stay the same, assuming that this was also God's desire, and they worked to ensure that happened.

Jeremiah's interpretation was radically different. In his famous temple sermon he tells the people, "Do not trust in deceptive words and say, This is the temple of the LORD, the temple of the LORD, the temple of the LORD!"[17] He then directs the people to look at Shiloh, where the Tabernacle had been situated. Its destruction by Yahweh showed that being the people of God did not bring protection from his judgement.[18]

Jeremiah was one of the few who saw that the problem went very deep and that it was not just an external problem. He

---

17 Jer 7:4.
18 c.f the expectation that God would ultimately intervene on behalf of his people in 3:3-5, 5:12, 14:7, 13 etc.

began to name the idolatries that people were blinded to, or that they did not see as being incompatible with faith in Yahweh. But, these problems were not limited to the religious sphere of life. For example, he exposed the corruption and oppression in economic life that had become accepted as part of the economic order. It seems that Jeremiah's awareness of the problems and their implications grew over time. It certainly was not an easy process for him, for he too had grown up within the system. At times he was at a loss as to God's response, accusing God of deceiving him. He saw that God was going to bring judgement in the form of exile, and that everything was going to change. In this he was radically different from those who remained blinded. But in another respect he was very like them, for while he knew things were going to change, he could not see how things would work out. He could not conceive how Israel could live as God's people without the temple and the land. He was confused when he looked to the future. He was not immune to the pain of the process. He had his own personal struggles with what God was doing and he himself grieved at the loss of the temple, land and the death of so many people.[19] Yet despite his confusion and uncertainty about how God would keep his promises to his people when their religious system, and even their existence, looked to be under threat, Jeremiah remained convinced that he would.[20] He was therefore able to prepare the people for the traumatic change that was coming.

If we are right in looking to the exile as a metaphor for our current situation, we must ask if we are in a similar state of shock and denial as Israel was when confronted with exile. We

---

19 See Jer 14:19-22 and 4:19, 8:18, 21-22, 15:10-21.
20 Jer 3:16-18, 16:14-15.

must seek to interpret the decline in church numbers and influence. We must ask hard questions about our church life, and we must face the possibility of a systematic corruption of which we are unaware simply because we are ourselves part of the system. The example of Jeremiah's time shows us that it is entirely possible to believe that we are faithfully worshipping God and that he will step in to turn the tide of events, when in fact the tide of events is his way of refining a corrupted people. It also warns us against assumptions about the structures of our church, the way in which we worship and the place of church in society. These have developed over hundreds of years and we can trace their development through history right back to the early church. It is almost natural, therefore, for us to assume that they are absolute and to struggle to imagine any other model. It is a simple step from this to assume that this model must continue, since God has indicated that the church is the primary instrument, sign and foretaste of the kingdom. Thus, we assume that God will at some stage step in to halt the decline of the church and restore its position in society. We may allow that minor corrections are necessary, but we are basically expecting, or perhaps longing for, a revival of things the way they were before.

It is by definition very difficult to become aware of the sort of institutional blindness that Jeremiah tried to communicate to his people. If our churches are suffering from a similar problem, then learning to see clearly is going to be a long and painful process. As was the situation in Jerusalem there will probably be a few prophets, who through various means, begin to question and wonder if things are not right. It is easy to assume that Jeremiah strode onto the scene from outside with a clear understanding of the system's problems, declaring

God's judgement on it and stating how things would work out. A close reading however shows that he was of a priestly family and so had himself grown up within the system. He was personally grieved that the way of worship he had grown up with would come to an end. He questioned God about what he was doing and was emotionally and physically hurt by the opposition he faced. We must also remember that when Jeremiah was speaking in Jerusalem it was by no means clear that his perspective was the right one. In fact the majority of opinion and almost all of the respected people within the religious institution were arguing the opposite, and they appeared to have good scriptural and theological reasons for doing so. It will be the same for those who feel that they must point out faults with the church now. They will share another problem with Jeremiah, in that they will be warning of great change, but they will not be able to articulate what things are going to look like after the change.

We must now address a crucial and difficult question. It is the question of what forms of institutional blindness the church in Britain might be suffering from. This is a difficult question to address for two reasons. First, as noted above, it is by definition very hard to become aware of your own blind-spots. Second, suggesting that there are problems in the church is profoundly unsettling for some people. Church is very closely tied with people's faith in, and experience of, God. Therefore, many find it hard to separate questioning of the church from questioning God himself. Becoming aware of blind-spots also necessarily involves a deep questioning and facing the possibility that I have been profoundly wrong, even if unintentionally. There is, therefore, an almost automatic reaction to deny what is suggested and to revert to the old, habitual and safe patterns of thought. The process is made even more difficult by the fact that those purporting to be exposing blind-spots will very seldom be indisputably right. Just as the truth of Jeremiah's prophecies only seem obvious from the standpoint of history, but at the time were far from indisputable, so now suggestions that the church has failed will be contested and the truth or otherwise of the suggestions will only become obvious over time. Not every criticism levelled at the church will be accurate and it requires discernment and courage to both be open to correction, while still discriminating between the various criticisms that inevitably come.

One of Jeremiah's chief criticisms of his people was about idolatry. It is clear that other gods were being worshipped alongside Yahweh, even in the official cult, which claimed to be Yahwist. It seems strange, but when Jeremiah pointed out this idolatry it was not denied and the people could not see any problem with it. This idolatry had crept in over a long period, with each generation growing up more and more used to having these other gods as part of the religious system. They seem to have abandoned a strict monotheism in favour of the view held by most of the world around them that different gods had different spheres of influence and were to be worshipped accordingly. According to this understanding worshipping a god for one area of life did not imply a sleight to another god with another sphere of influence. Each generation therefore grew up assuming that this sort of worship was not incompatible with their faith in Yahweh and could not see any incongruity in it. We must ask if it could be possible that some aspects of our church life and worship have become idolatrous in the same way. It is entirely possible that we have grown up assuming that certain things fit naturally alongside our worship of God, but in fact are idolatrous. Vinoth Ramachandra points out that idols can take the form of mental concepts as well as physical objects.[21] In fact behind every physical idol lies a mental concept which gives the idol its hold over us. Thus the worship of idols may not simply be expressed in the veneration of something out of a positive desire to worship it, but can also be expressed by living in fear of, or trying to appease, something seen to have ultimate control over life or parts of it. Such idols demand our worship in the sense that they demand our attention and effort because of the control or influence we perceive them to have over our lives. The attention and effort we give to these idols is not, therefore, available to God. Accepting this understanding of idolatry helps to uncover areas the modern church must seriously examine, in that it leads us to look for things which are perceived to have control or influence over our lives.

One area we must surely examine is that of economics, which has come to be attributed with godlike powers in our society. Ramachandra points out that money and 'the market' are human creations, yet the market has taken on 'semi-divine' status. It is seen to have power over nations and individuals, but it is not under their control. The market is spoken of as an independent reality. The idolatry of economics is much more than the danger of 'the love of money', it has to do with the acceptance of the worldview of economics, with its associated understanding of human nature, the problems experienced in the world and the correct way of dealing with them. Deep

---

21 Vinoth Ramachandra, *Gods That Fail: Modern Idolatry and Christian Mission* (Carlisle, Cumbria: Paternoster Press, 1996), p 107–110.

within economics lies an anthropology, an understanding and definition of humanity, which Ramachandra terms as the idol beginning to define us, to 're-create us in its image'. This leads to people and societies being assessed by their economic status and productivity. Market forces lead to policies which it is acknowledged will cause suffering and hardship to some, but which are deemed unavoidable because 'the market' dictates them. The same can be said of the gross inequalities within societies and throughout the world, which are justified and perpetuated by economic ideologies. Everyone recognises the problems, but there appear to be no alternatives, since this is what 'the market' dictates and no individual or government can change it. Thus, the violence of idolatry which Jeremiah spoke out against is repeated. In addition, it has been noted that 'economics is an imperialist beast',[22] in that its general approach is being applied to an increasingly wide range of human activity. This can be seen in the spread of the economic approach into areas such as health care and provision of services that traditionally had a different ethos. Given the widespread acceptance of this economic worldview in our society, and the fact that each of us is inextricably a part of the economic system, it would in fact be surprising if the church had avoided all influence by this worldview. The example of worship at the time of Jeremiah should alert us to the possibility that assumptions of the economic system have come to sit alongside and influence our faith and our church life so subtly that we have not been aware of it. Signs of this infection may be seen when the church delegates the economic sphere to those who are 'experts' in it, accepting violence done

---

22 I. R. L Harper and Samuel Gregg, *Christian Theology and Market Economics* (Cheltenham: Edward Elgar, 2008), p 87.

to people as unavoidable because of market forces. It may also be apparent in some of the models of mission and outreach, exemplified by a phrase I have often heard, 'mission costs money'. A certain model of mission may require money, and it fits with a Christendom model of church which is heavily dependent on buildings and staff. Yet, to move from this to state that 'mission needs money' is dangerously close to giving economics a sphere of influence alongside God. It leads to a dangerous paralysis, lack of imagination and insensitivity to the prompting of the Spirit in churches with limited financial resources. It also flies in the face of the experience of church history, which shows that significant missionary advances actually come through movements of God, often through the poor and vulnerable.

Another possible idol in the church is that of consumer choice, which is one of the fundamental aspects of life in the modern world. It has been pointed out that 'denominationalism is the religious aspect of secularization ... It is the social form in which the privatisation of religion is expressed'.[23] The denomination, or even the congregation, is a form of church which 'provides shelter for those who have made the same choice'[24] and 'the variety of denominations corresponds ... to the variety of brands available on the shelves of the supermarket'.[25] What we often forget is that the existence of denominations is relatively recent in the history of the church, and even more recent in the total history of God's people. The

---

23 Lesslie Newbigin, *Foolishness to the Greeks - the Gospel and Western Culture* (London: SPCK, 1986), p 145.

24 Ibid.

25 Lesslie Newbigin, *A Word in Season - Perspectives on Christian World Missions* (Grand Rapids, Michigan: Eerdmans, 1994), p 64.

assumption throughout the Old and New Testaments is that there is one body of God's people. In fact, part of the good news of the gospel is that not only does God in Christ overcome the alienation between himself and individuals, but equally the alienation between different individuals and peoples. The gospel is not primarily about the salvation of individuals, but God's purpose in Christ 'to reconcile to himself all things'.[26] The church is called to be the instrument, sign and foretaste of God's reign.[27] Part of what it is called to bring about, to point to and to give expression of is the reconciliation of people to God and each other in Christ. It simply cannot do this if 'it is itself the outward and visible form of an inward and spiritual surrender to the ideology of society'.[28] The questionable innovation of denominationalism is the existence of separate entities, none of which claim to be *the* Church, and who recognise each other as in some sense part of the universal church whilst maintaining separation from them. In contrast the position of the Orthodox and Roman Catholic traditions, that there is only one church, with the implication that the existence of 'separated brethren' remains a constant problem to be grappled with, has some

---

26 Col 1:20. Note: the gospel is not *primarily* about the salvation of individuals. God's overarching purpose is the reconciliation of *all things* to himself. This includes 'thrones, powers, rulers or authorities' (Col 1:16), which must include groupings of peoples. However, the reconciliation of groups of people with God, and then with each other, must begin with the reconciliation of individuals to God.

27 This is one of Newbigin's favourite descriptions of the church. See e.g. Newbigin, *A Word in Season - Perspectives on Christian World Missions*, p 60–5. for his explanation of it and how it shaped his ministry in inner-city Birmingham.

28 Ibid., p 64.

theological merit. Protestant denominations and independent churches have been   happy to co-exist with each other, basically operating as voluntary associations 'based on the free and personal choice of a number of individuals to cooperate for certain purposes'.[29] The historic denominations offer different options for worship and church polity based on disagreements and events several centuries ago. More and more new, independent congregations are being formed as believers honestly search for an expression of faith that fits with their experience in a world historical denominations struggle to relate to. The ecumenical movement may have been naïve in its quest for full reunification of the churches, yet surely the easy acceptance of increasing fragmentation is in complete contrast to Jesus' prayer, 'May they be brought to complete unity. Then the world will know that you sent me.'[30] The experience of exile may force a reassessment of the theology of denomination and church unity, as is already happening in some parts of Europe. For example, in my parents-in-law's town in Sweden their Mission Covenant Church congregation united with the Baptist congregation several years ago, and are now in talks to unite with the Methodist congregation.[31]

---

29 Newbigin, *Foolishness to the Greeks - the Gospel and Western Culture*, p 145.

30 John 17:23.

31 I am aware that this sort of union can be criticised for being driven by necessity and of downplaying the theological differences between the respective denominations. During my time as minister of a united Presbyterian and Methodist congregation I often heard the criticism that such unions were more about maintenance than mission. The point, however, is that in the crisis of exile, and the consequent struggle of the community of faith to survive, some crucial theological truths are

Identifying the idols which sit alongside God will be a painful and difficult process. Equally difficult will be the process by which we are weaned from our received and treasured understanding of what it is to be church. Jeremiah and his contemporaries naturally assumed that the temple, the priesthood and the nation of Israel living in its own land were essential for their existence as God's people. They had very strong historical and theological grounds for believing this. Most people probably recognised some faults with the system, but the total end to all three foundational elements predicted by Jeremiah would have been inconceivable. In a very similar way the church today is heavily centred on buildings and highly-qualified, salaried ministers. It has been used to existing in an environment where it shared the same worldview as the surrounding society. This gave it a role as the chaplain to society and at the same time allowed it to concentrate on the spiritual aspects of life and not give much consideration to other areas. These three elements are ingrained into our understanding of what it means to be church, so much so that we are as unable to imagine church without them as Jeremiah's contemporaries. We hold an unspoken assumption that if we are to fulfil God's calling to us as his people we must have influence, resources and expertise, pretty much as they assumed. There may also be an assumption that to be God's people is to have a certain privilege. The exile was an uncomfortable lesson that God's people are called to be the suffering servant to the nations. Perhaps we as the church today need to be reminded that the

---

forced to the surface, while others are shown to be less important than previously assumed.

Suffering Servant says 'as the Father sent me, I am sending you'.[32]

Jeremiah is a useful biblical model to consider in preparing for exile. The feelings of shock and denial evident in Jeremiah's contemporaries are familiar in churches facing changes in Britain. As the church faces up to these changes there will be different interpretations of the events. Some will argue that God will intervene to restore the church to its former position and success. The events are therefore to be resisted and the old ways are to be clung to. Some will argue that God is actually using the process, painful as it is, and the church must therefore be adaptable and receptive. The correct interpretation will only become obvious in many years time. While we are in the midst of events we have to weigh up the evidence, decide which interpretation we believe is right, and act accordingly.

---

32 John 20:21

Being in Exile: Anger and Depression

We have suggested that the appropriate metaphor for the church in the coming years is that of exile and that our first reaction to this is likely to be shock and denial. However, if we are correct, as time progresses we will be forced to move from assuming that God would not, or could not, allow this to happen to his church, to the realisation that it is happening. It will be the dawning realisation that that numbers are dropping, despite our best efforts to keep things going and our best attempts to attract people to our churches. The occasional 'success stories' will no longer be sufficient for us to ignore the truth as we see the closure of more and more churches which had been centres of witness for years. People who have believed God, trusted God and done their best, will find that things have not worked out. We will eventually realise that this is not a temporary blip, but likely to be the reality for the foreseeable future.

There will also be an increasing feeling of our own dislocation from society. Where the church once knew its place, and was accustomed to having a certain amount of influence, we will feel marginalised and powerless. We were used to a society that broadly accepted our worldview and values because of the symbiotic relationship between church and state that existed for hundreds of years. During this time the church felt it did not have to engage in depth with the surrounding culture, or the issues its members faced in their family and work lives. But as as the surrounding culture changes, and the value systems of church and society are no longer shared, the church will increasingly have to seriously engage with these areas. We will have to engage both in order to preserve the value systems within the church and in order to influence our society.

The symbiotic nature of the previous relationship between the church and the surrounding society, and the extent to which it has changed is highlighted in a recent judgement by Judge Andrew Rutherford, who stated, 'Whatever may have been the position in past centuries it is no longer the case that our laws must, or should automatically reflect the Judaeo-Christian position.'[33] In the past we were used to shaping public opinion on moral issues, now we find that we are a minority, barely tolerated and perhaps even coming into conflict with the courts.

Church closures, struggling congregations and loss of influence in society will lead to feelings of anger and depression. The anger may be directed in different ways, perhaps towards a denomination which is having to make difficult decisions about a closure, or toward God who has not stepped in to prevent it happening. It may be expressed toward the leadership in a congregation for not taking action to prevent decline. The depression may come in the form of a loss of confidence in the face of a secular society taking over the territory that once belonged to the church. It may come to those who were confident that the Lord would step in to turn things around, but now realise that revival is not coming. These experiences will throw up questions which cannot be avoided. Some will question God and the gospel, asking if it has proved inadequate to the challenges of the 21st century.

---

33 Andrew Brown, 'Why the Cornish Hotel Ruling Should Worry Conservative Christians', *Guardian.co.uk*, May 11, 2011, http://www.guardian.co.uk/commentisfree/andrewbrown/201 1/jan/18/cornish-hotel-ruling-conservative-christians.

Others may retain their confidence in the gospel and God's power, but ask what the reversal in fortunes of the church means. Has God withdrawn his blessing? Why?

The change curve suggests anger and depression as the feelings associated with this stage of a change process. Brueggemann says that the pastoral responsibility at this stage is to teach the people how to live in exile. What Brueggemann does not highlight is that the pastors themselves do not have a blueprint or prior experience of this. They will be seeking the answers to these big questions alongside the people they are leading, not from a position of prior experience. Some very foundational questions will have to be addressed, such as, How should we live, as God's people, in this situation? How much should we conform or not conform to this new society? Or, to put it in the terms of the psalmist, 'how can we sing the songs of the LORD while in a foreign land?'[34]

Once again it is useful to consider Israel's exile experience. We noted above the various conflicting interpretations of events in the period before the exile. Even after exile became a reality there was no consensus on how to understand what had happened and how to respond. When the first tranche of exiles were taken it was almost natural for those with a 'temple theology' to consider that those left in Jerusalem had been spared God's judgement. It was almost natural to think of those who had been taken as bearing the brunt of the judgement. According to Jeremiah, however, the opposite was true. It was those who had been taken into exile who God perceived to be 'good figs', whom he would watch over. Those remaining in Jerusalem were 'bad figs ... so bad that they

---

34 Psa 137:4.

cannot be eaten.'[35] Some confidently predicted a quick reversal in fortunes; that the exiles and articles removed from the temple would shortly be returned, because their temple theology demanded that God would 'break the yoke of the king of Babylon.'[36] Once again Jeremiah argued the opposite, telling the exiles to accept what had happened and to settle in the place in which they now found themselves. They were to adjust their mindset, to settle down and become productive citizens of this new land. Their faithfulness was to be shown in accepting their exile and not giving credence to those who would simply direct their attention back to the way things had been.[37]

The first chapters of Daniel give an insight as to how some responded to the experience of going into exile. Daniel and his companions were young men from a privileged background in Jerusalem, brought up within the dominant culture and theology centred on the temple, priesthood and kingdom. It is impossible to underestimate the trauma associated with their experience of the sacking of Jerusalem and forcible exile to a foreign land, where they did not know the language and culture. Not only were they psychologically vulnerable, but their entire faith and worldview had been thrown into question in the most violent way. This was a time of crisis for their faith and there were several alternative interpretations, each with implications for their approach to their situation. They could have concluded that Yahweh had been defeated and that Babylon and her gods had triumphed. They would then have completely assimilated into the Babylonian culture.

---

35 Jer 24:3, 5-7.
36 Jer 28:4 .
37 See Jer 29:1-23.

Another possible interpretation was that Yahweh had judged his people and abandoned them. This may have led to despair and withdrawal, or perhaps worshipping the Babylonian gods alongside Yahweh. They did not take either of these options. Rather, even in their emotionally and spiritually vulnerable state, they chose Jeremiah's option. They held on to the faith that, despite all the signs to the contrary, Yahweh was still in control, still faithful to his covenant and still to be worshipped. They chose to live faithful lives, even if it was no longer immediately apparent what a faithful life looked like. In Jerusalem, surrounded by a culture which shared a worldview which had Yahweh at the centre, the faithful life was well delineated. Now they were suddenly at the heart of an incredibly powerful culture, with different gods, values and morals. Not only this, but they were selected for service in the heart of this culture and enrolled in a programme to co-opt them into it.[38]

Those who have lived in another culture for a period of time will know that there are different strategies for coping with the tension between their own culture and the host culture. One option is rejection. It may be the host culture that is rejected as the person clings tenaciously to their own culture, refusing to change their clothing, eating habits etc. Or they may attempt to reject their home culture and totally conform to the host culture, although it is obviously impossible to obliterate all the influences and formative experiences of life. Rejection, therefore, is not a satisfactory response. Another

---

38 See Dan 1:4 where they were to be taught the 'language and literature of the Babylonians'. Language and literature are the primary vehicles for expressing the underlying traditions and values of a culture.

response is to attempt to compartmentalise the two cultures, so that at appropriate times they will conform to the host culture, but at other times live according to their home culture. However, life cannot be packaged into discrete units in this way and compartmentalising inevitably leads to problems and compromise. The most healthy strategy for living with two cultures is to allow a critical engagement between them. It is to be open to recognise the positive aspects of the host culture, and even allow them to expose hitherto unseen negative aspects of your own culture, and vice versa. This is a long term process, which is both enriching and challenging.

Daniel and his friend's decision to be faithful to Yahweh involved this sort of critical engagement. They chose not to attempt to reject their host culture, pagan as it was, nor to abandon their home faith and culture. Nor did they try to compartmentalise their faith into a small portion of their lives. In spite of their emotional and spiritual vulnerability, they chose to take the demanding option of critical engagement. The exercise of this critical engagement allowed them to be actively involved in their training programme and to assimilate large aspects of the host culture. There must have been many aspects of life in their new culture they had to adapt to. They inevitably made many compromises and changes in order to survive and thrive in the new environment.[39] Their spirit of critical engagement allowed for this, but it also led them to respectfully refuse the royal food as they did not want to defile themselves. We are not given any insight into why they decided not to compromise on this particular issue, nor the many hours of discussions they must

39 It would not have been possible, for example, to observe all of the purity laws while serving in the Babylonian civil service.

have had about the appropriate response to this and other areas of conflict between the cultures. They not only had to negotiate which parts of the host culture to accept or reject, but they had to find new ways of worship. Previously, in Jerusalem, their relationship with God was centred on the temple and the priesthood. These were no longer available, so they had to explore new ways of worship, consonant with all that had gone before but appropriate to the new reality.

The exiles were thrown into a strange, new culture and had to negotiate their relationship to it. It was a totally new situation for them as a community of faith and there was no blue-print as to the exact shape their life of faith should take within it. We should, therefore, not be surprised to see variations in approach as different individuals and groups of exiled Israelites grappled with the issues. Daniel and his friends felt it necessary to draw clear boundary lines on certain issues. The exiles in Susa seem not to have drawn any such lines, to the extent that Esther is expressly encouraged to hide her Jewish background, and seems to have no problem in becoming part of Xerxes' harem.[40] It is not hard to imagine that if Daniel and Esther had met a rather heated discussion about the appropriate way of life for Israelites in exile and appropriate levels of adaptation to the host culture would have ensued! Daniel (and his community) could have accused Esther (and her community) of having compromised too much and not being faithful enough. Esther could have accused Daniel of holding on to laws which were simply not relevant in the new context and of exclusivity. What this highlights again, is the fact that there is no blue-print for the faithful life in exile. It is a new situation which previous tradition, and

---

40 Est 2:10.

even the scriptures, do not explicitly address. The outlines of the faithful life will be drawn from these sources, and must be consistent with them, but will only emerge through discussion, debate and even argument as issues arise. In Jerusalem the faithful life was easily defined, but in exile various communities found different expressions and emphasised different things. It will be the same for us as we enter exile, and there will inevitably be disagreements and arguments over the various approaches. The only certainty is that the old certainties have gone.

Yet, despite their differences, both Daniel's and Esther's communities are shown to have ultimately shared the same basic loyalty to Yahweh. They were living at the heart of an empire whose attitude toward the faiths of their peoples swung between tolerance and intolerance. The Israelites in exile were constantly under pressure, but there were moments of intense crisis. These crises centred on the question of ultimate loyalty. Mordecai refused to bow down to Haman, because his loyalty to God and his people would not allow him to. Daniel and his friends refused to show their loyalty to the empire by bowing down to the god of the empire, or the emperor himself. Despite their different approaches to the host culture, when their ultimate loyalty was questioned the community of faith was unambiguous in its response. The empire could not ignore such disloyalty and turned its power against those who confessed a different allegiance. At such times the community was at its weakest and most vulnerable, with its very existence hanging in the balance. Yet it was at these times that they spoke most powerfully to the host culture.

Prophets in Jerusalem, such as Jeremiah and Isaiah, had a certain authority which allowed them to speak to the religious and political establishment, even if what they said was not popular. The close relationship between the religious and political structures allowed for the role of the prophet and even allowed access to those in authority. In exile prophets of Yahweh had no such authority or rights. The state had its own advisers and was not open to the wisdom of an apparently defeated and discredited god. It is true that Daniel and his companions brought the word of the Lord to the emperor. He was profoundly affected by them, culminating in his decree 'that in every part of my kingdom people must fear and reverence the God of Daniel.'[41] But this only occurred when they were at their weakest and most vulnerable, having shown their ultimate loyalty was to God, not the empire. The story of Esther concludes with many people of other nationalities becoming Jews,[42] but once again this only happened after Mordecai and Esther's ultimate loyalty had been exposed as being, not to the empire, but to Yahweh, and they had been threatened with extinction. Israel's purpose, to be a blessing to the nations, was not fulfilled in the period of power, prestige and prosperity. Rather, it began to be fulfilled in the time when Israel was weak, lacking influence and itself struggling to discern how to worship and live faithful lives in a new context.

This brief exploration of the exile's experience highlights several lessons for the modern church entering exile. First, we must interpret the trends facing the church correctly. The figures of decline are incontestable, but the correct response

---

41 Dan 6:26.
42 Est 8:17.

requires a true interpretation. An ecclesiology and missiology that sees strong and influential churches as crucial to God's purposes will necessarily argue for some sort of revival, perhaps after a period of 'testing' or 'purifying'. This is an attractive and easy option, for it demands very little real change. However, if revival does not come it will lead to anger, depression and a crisis of faith. If the metaphor of exile is appropriate, then the decline in numbers and loss of influence of the church is a disciplining and purifying process, and the experience of exile is to be entered into. Like Daniel and his community the church must not look back, nor envy the few 'successful' churches who appear to have escaped the exile experience. Rather it must take the difficult decision to critically engage with the new context whilst deciding to live a faithful life. The problem is that, as in the experience of Israel, it is not yet obvious which interpretation is correct.

Second, the primary requirement of the church is faithfulness. The experience of exile is bound to result in feelings of vulnerability and uncertainty. Yet it is in this state of weakness that the church, like Daniel and his companions, is to take the decision to live a radically faithful life. Although we have argued that the early church period is not the best metaphor for the church at this time, it is instructive to consider Paul's instructions to new churches. As Roland Allen pointed out, Paul had a strategy of planting churches in strategic centres of population, expecting that they would act as centres for the planting of churches in that area.[43] It is very striking, therefore, to note that in his letters to the churches there is almost no encouragement or instruction about this strategic purpose. There are no exhortations for the churches to organise

---

43 Allen, *Missionary Methods - St Paul's or Ours?*, p 10–17.

evangelistic campaigns, or to plant churches in their area. Instead, the letters are exhortations and explanations about faithful living to small communities of faith in the context of the Roman empire; faithfulness incorporating doctrine and practice. It appears that Paul placed primary importance on faithful living and assumed that mission would then follow naturally.

Third, in the new context we cannot simply assume that the shape of the faithful life will be the same as that of the previous era. Just as Daniel and Esther simply could not continue to worship and live as had been possible in Jerusalem, so old patterns of the Christian life will become unsustainable in the new context. This may happen because society changes in such ways as to make certain things impracticable, or because new moral or ethical challenges arise which have simply never arisen before.

Fourth, there will be debate, and even disagreement, over the appropriate response to these changes and challenges. Some will demand that faithfulness means making as few compromises as possible to the traditional pattern of Christian life, while others will argue that larger parts of the traditional pattern are merely tradition. The process of moving into exile will force the church to engage with a society and culture that has changed, and is changing, in a way that it has not had to for centuries. The search for a meaningful description of the faithful life may have a particular impact on the historical denominations. The distinctive theologies, structures and practices of these denominations lie in the disputes of a different era. As the church is forced to grapple with the shape of the faithful life in the new context people from different denominations will find common ground in their approach to certain issues. At the same time, within denominations there will be disagreements about the appropriate responses. There will thus be a drawing together across denominations and divisions of approach within them. A diversity of responses is to be expected, not as a capitulation to the spirit of the age of post-modernism, but simply because the church is in a situation where it is exploring and developing new forms appropriate to a new situation.

Fifth, living a faithful life will inevitably lead to occasions of conflict with the reigning worldview. The church may not be going into exile into a literal empire, but as is frequently noted there is an imperial aspect to modern worldviews. For example, a recent report has stated:

> We speak of Empire, because we discern a coming together of economic, cultural, political and military power in our world today, that constitutes a reality and a spirit of lordless domination, created by humankind yet enslaving simultaneously; an all-encompassing global reality serving, protecting and defending the interests of powerful corporations, nations, elites and privileged people, while imperiously excluding even sacrificing humanity and exploiting creation; a pervasive spirit of destructive self-interest, even greed - the worship of money, goods and possessions; the gospel of consumerism, proclaimed through powerful propaganda and religiously justified, believed and followed; the colonization of consciousness, values and notions

of human life by the imperial logic; a spirit lacking in compassionate justice and showing contemptuous disregard for the gifts of creation and the household of life.[44]

Empires may have differing attitudes towards religion, but at their heart they demand the loyalty of their subjects. Both Daniel and the early church lived in empires which tolerated, and even encouraged, the different religions of their peoples. However, they also demanded an equal expression of loyalty to the empire itself, in the form of worship to the emperor. Most religions had no problems in putting loyalty to the state alongside loyalty to their gods, and the state saw this as an expression of the contract between it and the people.[45] In a similar way the idealogical empires surrounding the modern church in exile are happy for their citizens to have their religions, as long as they recognise the empire's authority in its

---

44 Council for World Mission, 'CWM Theology Statement 2010', *CWM: A Partnership of Churches in Mission*, May 23, 2011, http://www.cwmission.org/theological-papers/cwm-theology-statement-2010.

45 See the reaction of Celsus when Christians refused to swear an oath to the Roman emperor:

> 'Even if someone is told to take an oath by an emperor among men, that is also nothing dreadful. For earthly things have been given to him, and whatever you receive in this life you receive from him … if you overthrow this doctrine, it is probable that the emperor will punish you. If everyone were to do the same as you, there would be nothing to prevent him from being abandoned, alone and deserted, while earthly things would come into the power of the most lawless and savage barbarians.'

J. Stevenson, *A New Eusebius: Documents Illustrating the History of the Church to AD 337* (SPCK, 1995), p 135–6.

realm. Thus economic and other theories are seen to be autonomous within their spheres and the claims of religion are simply not recognised as applicable. The church will run into problems when it refuses, as it must, to relegate its loyalty to God to one small area of life. It will come into conflict with many of the most powerful ideologies of this age and will be doing so from a position of weakness, not strength. It may appear that the church will inevitably be crushed by these forces, yet it is in these times that the church will be speaking prophetically and will find that God's mission can progress even when, or perhaps especially when, the church is at its most vulnerable.

Departing From Exile: Acceptance and Integration

The move from being the church in Christendom to a church living in cultural exile will be painful. It will involve periods of shock and denial moving to depression and anger. Yet the church will eventually move to a new stage of acceptance and integration. We will move from wondering if it is even possible to sing the Lord's song in a strange land to composing songs of worship in the rhythms and idioms of the new land. This is the stage of accepting all that has happened, recognising the Lord's hand in it, and integrating it into our experience, life and worship.

Jeremiah encouraged the people to settle in exile, to accept it as a reality and to seek the benefit of the society of which they became a part. Daniel and Esther, along with Ezekiel and others, worked through their feelings of depression and anger and ultimately found ways to live faithful lives in a very new context. Daniel and his companions had faithfulness at the fore from the beginning, while it seems that Esther, Mordecai and their community only discovered their faithfulness when their existence as a community was being threatened.

A new period began for the people with the decree of Cyrus, which allowed the Jews to return to their own land. Once again they were faced with choices which had no obvious answers. Many decided to stay in the communities which had become home to them. Others decided to return to the land of their ancestors, to the land of promise. Many of these were probably hoping that this marked a return to the way things had been before. Nehemiah's prayer and his words to the emperor give voice to the continuing connection with

Jerusalem and their hopes for the future.[46] When Zerubbabel and other exiles returned to Jerusalem and work on rebuilding the temple began, it was a moment of both great joy and great poignancy.[47] Later, there was great excitement when Ezra brought back the articles used for worship in the temple. Yet, despite the people's hopes, this was not to be a return to things as they had been. The experience of exile had profoundly changed them as a people and, even though they were returning to their own land, they would never again be truly free from the influence of empire. Even though they were once again living in their own land, with the temple and priesthood functioning again, there was a profound feeling that, 'although she had come back from Babylon, the glorious message of the prophets remained unfulfilled'[48] and the exile was not really over.[49]

In spite of this continuing feeling of marginalisation, the Jewish people began to accept the experience of exile and integrate it into their faith. Brueggeman lists some of the facets of this post-exilic model.[50] First, the community of faith had to live in a context in which it had little influence over the public policy of the empire. Second, there were constant temptations to cultural syncretism, as shown in the Maccabean period by Jewish boys trying to hide evidence of their circumcision.[51] There was a constant temptation for people to adopt the norms of whichever empire was in control, with the

---

46 Neh 1:5-11, 2:3.
47 Ezr 3:12-13.
48 Wright, *The New Testament and the People of God*, p 269.
49 see, e.g. Neh 9:36-37.
50 Brueggemann and Miller, *A Social Reading of the Old Testament - Prophetic Approaches to Israel's Communal Life*, p 269–272.
51 Wright, *The New Testament and the People of God*, p 158.

concurrent danger of the community losing its distinct identity. Third, in the face of political irrelevance and social syncretism the community had to work very hard to maintain its distinct identity. It did this in three ways. First, it worked at developing a strong feeling of connection between the current community and its history. There is evidence that most of the genealogies of the Old Testament belong to this period. The genealogies not only served to legitimise a person's place in the community, but to link them to the 'reference points from the past.'[52] Second, when faced with a situation that could lead to despair the community intentionally practised hope. Apocalyptic literature, with its bizarre imagery, became a common form of deliberately expressing hope during this time. To communities that had been marginalised by the power of empire, apocalyptic literature enabled people to see beyond their immediate hopeless situation to the realities being played out in the spiritual realm. Through apocalyptic literature the community was responding to a situation which would appear to lead inevitably to despair by intentionally and deliberately filling their imagination with the concrete promises of God. The third strategy the community used to maintain its identity was by becoming a textual community. This was the period in which the canon of the Old Testament was formed, but it was also a period when the community was engaged in interpreting the text. Brueggemann highlights the emergence of the synagogue, the formation of the Beth Midrash ('the house of study') and the eventual emergence of the rabbis as teachers of the tradition. The community of faith after the exile looked very different from that which had gone

---

52 Brueggemann and Miller, *A Social Reading of the Old Testament - Prophetic Approaches to Israel's Communal Life*, p 271.

before. Looking into the future before the exile it would have been impossible to see the future shape of the community and its life of faith, but looking back it is possible to see the lines of continuity as well as differences.

It is also worth noting that in returning to their foundational traditions and texts the exilic and post-exilic communities were doing so in a very creative manner. Their history and traditions were not something that restricted them, but were to be reinterpreted for the new context. For instance, it is widely accepted that the material of the Pentateuch was reinterpreted by the exilic community. An example can be seen in the stories of creation in Genesis 1 and 2, which appear to have been used to directly challenge the worldview assumptions of the empires of the Ancient Near East.[53] The history of 1 and 2 Kings was also re-written in the form of 1 and 2 Chronicles. These books tell the same story, but place emphasis on different aspects according to the pastoral purpose of the writers. Thus 1 and 2 Kings describe the failures of the people, and so give an explanation for the exile. 1 and 2 Chronicles place less emphasis on the failings of the people, but rather emphasise God's covenant promises to them, giving hope for the future.

Perhaps the greatest creativity in using the scriptures came later, in the post-exilic period, with the decision of the

---

53 Howard Peskett and Vinoth Ramachandra, *The Message of Mission - The Glory of Christ In All Time and Space* (Leicester: Inter-Varsity Press, 2003), p 33–36. Brueggemann and others argue that Gen 1 and 2 were written 'as a liturgical assertion against the temptations of the Babylonian gods in exile' (Walter Brueggemann, *Theology of the Old Testament: Testimony, Dispute, Advocacy* (Minneapolis: Fortress Press, 2005), p 153.

diaspora communities to translate them into the languages of the nations they were living among. Language is arguably the most fundamental element of a worldview. Drawing from his many years of missionary experience Lesslie Newbigin points out that 'traditions of rationality are embodied in languages.'[54] If there is to be a meaningful encounter between two traditions of rationality then one must move beyond simply looking for words and phrases which correspond as closely as possible to those in the other language. Translation is not simply the matching up of equivalent words, but involves the translation of concepts from one idiom to another.[55] Again drawing from his missionary experience in India, Newbigin describes how the simple introduction of Jesus to those who have never heard his name demands some explanation of who he is.[56] Options in the Indian languages included Swamy ('Lord'), Satguru (the true teacher), Avatar (incarnation of God) or Kadaval (the transcendent God). The problem is that each of these 'necessarily place Jesus within a world of ideas that is formed by the Hindu tradition and that is embodied in the language of the people.'[57] It is impossible to avoid the use of terms which already carry a weight of meaning, and yet 'the introduction of the name of Jesus places the structure under a strain it cannot bear without breaking.'[58] Newbigin's analysis

54 Lesslie Newbigin, *The Gospel in a Pluralist Society* (Grand Rapids, Michigan: Eerdmans, 1989), p 55.

55 For example, in Britain the word 'dog' most often has positive connotations of a household pet. In many societies the word had connotations of a scavenging animal to be avoided.

56 Lesslie Newbigin, *The Open Secret - An Introduction to the Theology of Mission* (Grand Rapids, Michigan: Eerdmans, 1995), p 19–20.

57 Ibid., p 20.

58 Ibid.

highlights the dangers involved in the decision to translate the scriptures into the languages of the empire, for 'every translation involves a fresh interpretation'.[59] It is for this reason that Islam teaches that the Qur'an can only be heard in Arabic and should not be translated.

The re-interpreting of the ancient tradition in a new and different way, allied with the translation of the texts themselves, shows a remarkable creativity. It was a creativity that was both necessary for survival, but more importantly a creativity that is inherent in God's promise and purpose that Israel would be a blessing to the nations. The crisis of the exile caused the community to come together in order to survive, to look back to their defining texts and to appropriate these in the new context. Out of this came a new form to their life and worship; a new shape to the faithful life. It was a form that could not have been predicted beforehand, while they were still resident in Jerusalem. Yet looking back clear lines of continuity could be seen. It was a paradigm shift.

This creativity in re-interpreting the life of faith into new contexts is now a crucial responsibility of the church. The story of redemption has been described as an drama with six acts.[60] Act I is creation, where the Author's intentions are revealed and the scene is set. Act II, the fall, is the crime where tension is introduced and relationships are broken. The rest of the story is about the resolution of the tension. Act III is the story of Israel and Act IV is the story of Jesus, 'the decisive, pivotal act that begins to unravel the plot conflict at its deepest

---

59 Newbigin, *The Gospel in a Pluralist Society*, p 185.
60 B. J Walsh and S. C Keesmaat, *Colossians Remixed: Subverting the Empire* (Milton Keynes: Paternoster, 2005), p 133–4.

roots.'[61] Act VI is the final act in which the Author's purposes are finally realised. Between Acts IV and VI comes Act V, the story of the church. But early in this act the script breaks off. There is 'no canonically established script that gets us from the beginning of Act V to the final Act VI.'[62] The church is called to 'develop the imaginative skills necessary to improvise on this cosmic stage of creational redemption.'[63] This improvisation must be done within certain parameters. It must be faithful to the story which has gone before, and it must be deliberately heading toward the finale as it has been shown to us. It must also be faithful to the promptings of the Holy Spirit, who has been given as our Director. Thus the task of the church in Act V is faithful improvisation. It cannot simply keep on repeating earlier parts of the script, nor can it branch off in a direction bearing no relation to what has gone before, or which is not in line with the finale that has been revealed.

This faithful improvisation can be seen in the life of the early church. The extent of improvisation is evident in the events around Jerusalem Council in Acts 15. The church was facing a situation for which it had no precedent and for which the tradition provided no specific guidance. Large numbers of gentiles were coming to faith, raising the question of the terms by which they were to be accepted into membership. The early church saw itself as continuous with, even the fulfilment of, the people of Israel, so it was natural to assume that gentile converts would have to be circumcised to join the community of faith. From the standpoint of history it is hard for us to understand the force of the argument for circumcision. It was

61 Ibid., p 133.
62 Ibid.
63 Ibid., p 134.

the God-given sign of membership of God's people and had never previously been questioned. While Jesus had made comments that in some ways relativised the food laws, he had made no such comments about circumcision. Those arguing for circumcision appeared to have both scripture and the teaching of Jesus on their side. Those arguing against argued simply on the basis that the gentiles had been given the Holy Spirit, which demonstrated God's acceptance of them in Christ. In other places Paul argues that this move is in line with the trajectory set by Jesus and God's ultimate purposes in reconciling all peoples to himself.[64] Dropping the requirement for circumcision was an act of improvisation in the face of a new situation. Once again we see that the right course of action was by no means clear, but was a matter of great debate. It is also important to note that the decision of the council did not come out of the blue, but was part of the process of dealing with a controversy that had been brewing since the incident with Peter and Cornelius. Also, the simple fact that a decision had been reached at the council did not mean that all debate and tension was over. The decision of the council is an example of the sort of radical improvisation that is required in order to be faithful at times when merely 'faithfully' repeating earlier parts of the script would in fact be an act of unfaithfulness.

However, it must be remembered that improvisation must be faithful improvisation. Improvisation does not mean total licence, which is a fear that those who are comfortable within an established system often express. Improvisation in music is

---

64 But these arguments developed within the early church as a response to the giving of the Spirit to the gentiles. Such arguments were not conceivable before then.

not the mere sounding of random notes by a child, but the skilful expression of an accomplished musician. It demands close attention to the tempo, rhythm and mood of the music, otherwise it will be disharmonious. It is the blend of training and practice in the theory of chord progressions and harmonies with the inspiration of the music that is happening now. The church's improvisation must come out of a similar immersion in its story, if its response to its environment is not to be discordant with the rest of the drama.

The necessity of improvisation confirms what we noted when looking at Daniel and Esther: that we should not be surprised when communities of faith express the life of faith in different ways. This can also be seen in the New Testament. Consider another live issue for the early church living in the heart of a multi-faith empire. One thing all Christians were agreed on was that there was only one God and that no other god could be worshipped. The debate was over whether Christians could eat meat that might previously have been used in idolatrous ceremonies. Such meat might be on sale in the market or served at a dinner party. This may not be a live issue for Christians in the West, but similar issues arise, for example, in the church in Nepal, surrounded as it is by a Hindu culture. It is impossible for the church as a small minority to cut off all contact with the surrounding culture, yet there is a strong desire to avoid all appearance of honouring Hindu gods. There is thus much debate, often heated, about what is, or is not, acceptable for Christians. This sort of debate is increasing in Nepal as the number of second-generation Christians increases. First-generation converts often make a total break with almost every aspect of their former culture and religion. Second-generation Christians often have a more nuanced view of the culture and religion, and argue that it is unnecessary to shun practices which they perceive as purely cultural. These debates, in the early church and in Nepal, are often heated because they touch on a fundamental issue: that worship should be given to God alone. Surely if any issue should have protective guidelines set up to prevent Christians from falling into error, it is this. Yet Paul does not take this line. Instead he restates the agreed principles about God and idols,[65] but moves on to argue for acceptance of different interpretations of the implications. Some will not feel it right to eat, others will feel it is right.[66] There is to be respect between those who hold the different views. Those with a 'strong' conscience are not to use it in such a way as to cause problems for those with 'weak' consciences.[67] Perhaps the harder part is for those who think that eating such meat is idolatrous. They are not to judge those who do, but to trust that they are acting out of faithfulness to God.[68] The upshot is that each person is called to be 'fully convinced in their own mind' and to 'stop passing judgement on one another.'[69] Even on this subject, which touched on one of the most central tenets of faith, diversity was to be accepted, not in the doctrine, but in the way it was outworked into a life of faith.

Act V of God's drama, the period of the church, demands the church to improvise, under the guidance of the Holy Spirit as director, toward the conclusion of the drama. The script will not, however, continue at a constant pace. There will be times

---

65 1 Cor 8:4-6.
66 1 Cor 8:7-8.
67 1 Cor 8:9-13.
68 Rom 14:3-4.
69 Rom 14:5, 13.

when the drama seems to move at a quicker pace. Hans Küng notes how the church has gone through several paradigm shifts throughout its history. The concept of paradigm shift is drawn from Thomas Khun's work on the philosphy of science. He argued that each branch of science works with a model, or paradigm, with which it understands its field. This model, e.g. Newtonian physics, is generally held to explain and predict what happens in the world. Over time problems accumulate as data emerges that does not fit with the model. As more anomalous data emerges the existing model is increasingly seen to be inadequate and some pioneers search for a new model. Eventually a new model is found, which encompasses the knowledge of the old, but also explains the data which could not be fitted within it. Thus the Einsteinian paradigm superseded the Newtonian. Within the old paradigm it was not possible to predict the new, but looking back it is possible to see the lines of continuity. Küng argues that a similar process has operated throughout church history.[70] As the environment around the church changes so more and more areas of mismatch between the current church model and its environment become apparent. This results in a crisis, but for the old model to be replaced there needs to be 'a worthy, credible model to succeed it.'[71] Times of paradigm shift are, therefore, by definition, unsettling. They are times when old certainties are thrown up in the air and it is not at all clear what new certainties, if any, will take their place. As Küng

---

70 Küng argues on the basis of paradigm changes in theology, but the paradigm changes he notes have as many socio-political factors as theological. See Hans Küng, *Theology for the Third Millennium: An Ecumenical View* (London: Harper Collins, 1991), p 123–169.

71 Ibid., p 144.

notes, they will be times when we experience doubt, and the search for a new paradigm will involve a whole range of objective and subjective factors. As a new model emerges it will initially have 'few and mostly young advocates' and acceptance of it will require 'something like a conversion' for those accustomed to the old one.[72] This is a difficult process for many, with the result that there continues to be resistance to the new model for many years. Max Planck's comment about physicists holds true for the church: 'A new scientific truth tends to win acceptance not because its opponents become convinced and declare their conversion, but rather because the opponents gradually die out and the upcoming generation has already become familiar with the truth.'[73]

I have been arguing that the church is in the midst of such a time of paradigm change. The Christendom models of church are being put under increasing strain as the environment around it is changing. I have also argued that exile is the appropriate biblical metaphor to guide us through this experience. Küng's analysis of paradigm shifts in church history warns us that this will be a long process. There will be those who look back with nostalgia, since the attitude of Christendom 'continues mentally in the attitudes and aspirations of the church' because the church has 'created for itself a position to preserve or, in our case, regain.'[74] Others, probably generally younger people, as Küng notes, will engage with the the confusing and uncertain task of faithful

---

72 Ibid., p 148–9.
73 Ibid., p 150.
74 Thomas F Foust et al., *A Scandalous Prophet - the Way of Mission After Newbigin*, ed. Thomas F Foust et al. (Grand Rapids, Michigan: Eerdmans, 2002), p 34.

improvisation. For us, as for the Jewish exiles, this will require a fresh look at previous assumptions about what it is to be the people of God, coupled with a turn to the ancient traditions to find resources from which to draw. For the Jews this was not an intellectual exercise, but was driven by harsh circumstances and the question of survival. It is no different for us, since 'it is the questions about who we are and what we are for that exile provokes most.'[75]

We have seen that the pre-exilic and Christendom models shared an emphasis on a building or buildings, a highly specialised and trained clergy and formalised and structured forms of worship. Each of these elements demand significant resources and finance, and are thus suited to a situation where the community of faith has a dominant position in society. Although the church has not yet entered the stage of acceptance and integration, that is to say the new paradigm has not yet emerged, it is necessary to ask if there are any signs that it might be emerging. Two current movements within the British church illustrate the process of exploration that is going on.

First, the Northumbria community. This community is made up of 'hugely diverse people, from different backgrounds, streams and edges of the Christian faith' committed 'to embrace and express an ongoing exploration into a new way for living Christianly - a way that offers hope in the changed and changing culture of today's world.'[76] The community has deliberately looked back to ancient traditions to find the

---

75 Ibid., p 35.
76 The Northumbria Community, 'Who Are We? Well, Let's Begin Here...', *The Northumbria Community*, June 22, 2011, http://www.northumbriacommunity.org/who-we-are.

resources for this exploration, particularly the Celtic and monastic traditions. In this they have been inspired by a quotation from Bonhoeffer:

> 'The renewal of the church will come from a new type of monasticism which only has in common with the old an uncompromising allegiance to the Sermon on the Mount. It is high time men and women banded together to do this.'[77]

The community is founded on a Rule of Vulnerability and Availability. Availability is to be towards God, through the devotional life expressed in the 'cell' of the heart and the use of the 'daily office'.[78] Availability to others is expressed in the practice of hospitality, intercession and mission. Vulnerability involves accountability and being teachable. It also involves embracing the 'heretical imperative', that is, 'speaking out when necessary or asking awkward questions that upset the status quo; by making relationships the priority, and not reputation.'[79] Vulnerability also leads to seeking to live as the

---

77 Ibid. It is interesting to note that this quotation has also inspired the establishment of various other new monastic communities. See, for example, S. Claiborne, *The Irresistible Revolution: Living as an Ordinary Radical* (Zondervan, 2008). and Andy Freeman, *Punk Monk* (Eastbourne: Survivor, 2004).

78 The 'daily office' is the term given to the four set times of prayer observed at the mother house of the Northumbria Community, and which companions of the community are encouraged to follow as appropriate to the schedule of their daily lives. See Northumbria Community and Northumbria Community Staff, *Celtic Daily Prayer*, p 12.

79 The Northumbria Community, 'Building the New on Foundations of Old', *The Northumbria Community*, June 22, 2011, http://www.northumbriacommunity.org/sharing-wisdom/347-building-the-new-on-foundations-of-old?showall=1.

'church without walls', 'living openly amongst unbelievers and other believers in a way that the life of God in ours can be seen, challenged or questioned.'[80] Central to this task are the three questions the community, individually and corporately, seek to answer: 'who is it that you seek?', 'how then shall we live?' and 'how shall we sing the Lord's song in a strange land?' From very small beginnings in the late 1970's and early 80's the community has grown so that the 'mother house' in Northumbria is now the centre of a network of groups throughout the UK, Holland, France, Canada and the USA. It is an example of faithful improvisation in the face of the changing environment the church is encountering. The questions raised by this challenge have drawn together people from various denominational backgrounds, along with people who have struggled to relate to traditional church structures. In seeking an appropriate model the community has deliberately turned to the history of the church for resources, but have moulded and adapted them to the reality of their current situation. The resulting model represents a clear departure from the Christendom emphasis on buildings, clergy and programmes.

The second example is of an historic denomination's engagement with the journey into exile. In 2004 the Church of England produced the 'Mission-shaped Church' report.[81] The report was written to assess progress in church planting and consider new developments. In doing so it devoted

---

80 Ibid.
81 Working Group of Church of England's Mission and Public Affairs Council, *Mission-shaped Church - Church Planting and Fresh Expressions of Church in a Changing Context* (London: Church House Publishing, 2004).

considerable attention to the changes in British society and their effects on the church. It noted that there were now several categories of people within British society: the churched, the de-churched and the non-churched. De-churched people are those who have had a connection with a church, but have drifted away from it. An increasingly large proportion of society is non-churched, never having had a meaningful connection with a church. The distinction between de-churched and non-churched is important for the church to recognise. The report recognises that there have been many creative responses to the changed context. These are termed 'fresh expressions' of church and include alternative worship communities, cell churches, café churches and network focussed churches, amongst others. The emergence of these fresh expressions leads on to a chapter looking at theology for a missionary church, showing a willingness to probe below the surface issues of structure and organisation to re-examine the very nature of the church. The final two chapters deal with methodologies for developing fresh expressions, and working towards an enabling framework within the denomination. Within four years of its publication the report had become the biggest selling report produced by the Church of England[82] and several books on the 'mission-shaped' theme had been published.[83] The ongoing reflection on these themes continued

---

82 E. S Croft and S. J.L Croft, *Mission Shaped Questions: Defining Issues for Today's Church* (London: Church House Publishing, 2008), p 2.

83 For example, S. Gaze, *Mission-Shaped and Rural: Growing Churches in the Countryside* (London: Church House Publishing, 2006); Margaret Withers, *Mission-Shaped Children: Moving Towards a Child-Centred Church* (London: Church House Publishing, 2006); P. Bayes, T. Sledge, and J. Holbrook, *Mission-*

to be developed in response to the creative initiatives of people throughout Britain, who were seeking to find expressions of faith appropriate to their context. A Fresh Expressions network has been established with an active website featuring stories from around Britain.[84] The network also offers publications and training. The Mission-shaped Church report and the Fresh Expressions movement show how one denomination has faced the challenge of exile. It has involved a re-imaging of the church and its structures and creative improvisation accompanied by new theological reflection on basic issues. It is unsurprising that it has its critics. Hull, for example, has questioned if the movement has not acquiesced to the consumer culture in arguing for varied forms of church, rather than offering a critique of the culture.[85]

Shaped Parish: Traditional Church in a Changing Context (London: Church House Publishing, 2006); S. Hope, *Mission-Shaped Spirituality: The Transforming Power of Mission* (London: Church House Publishing, 2006); I. J Mobsby, *Emerging and Fresh Expressions of Church: How Are They Authentically Church and Anglican?* (London: Moot Community Publishing, 2008).

84 'Changing Church for a Changing World | Fresh Expressions', *Fresh Expressions,* February 13, 2012, http://www.freshexpressions.org.uk/.

85 J. Hull, *Mission-Shaped Church: A Theological Response* (London: SCM Press, 2006), p 19, 25.

Conclusion

At the start of this essay I related how my thinking on the theme of exile was sparked by a conversation with Roy Searle. The concept of exile being the appropriate metaphor for the church in Britain immediately resonated with me, and demanded further exploration. The process has confirmed to me that this metaphor provides insights, challenges and guidance for the British church in what is a challenging and unsettling period of transition. Since my main reason for writing has been to explore this in relation to my own life and ministry I conclude with some personal reflections.

Studying the metaphor of exile has helped me locate myself, both personally and as the minister of a congregation belonging to a historical denomination. Personally, I identify with the feeling of being an exile. I belong to a community of faith, the Presbyterian Church in Ireland, which is part of the wider community of faith, the church. This community of faith has nurtured me and formed me in many ways, and I feel a great loyalty and commitment to it. Yet, I have an underlying feeling of frustration and longing for something more. It is a frustration and longing that stems from a mismatch I feel between the spirituality, forms of worship and structure of the church and the world that I live in. It feels like we are trying to trying to carry on the worship of Jerusalem when we have already been deported to Babylon. I am looking for a spirituality that is robust enough to engage with a world that has changed around the church. I want to worship in ways that connect me with the long and rich history of the community of faith, both within my own tradition and beyond, but that also connects with the cultural idiom that has become my home. I am attracted to some of the principles expressed by the alternative worship community, when they say that the 'appropriation of tradition was to be playful as well as serious and eclectic as well as respectful.'[86] Of course I am not merely looking for a spirituality that expresses worship in a way that is appropriate to my cultural context, but which connects me with the God who is sovereign. Because he is sovereign the spirituality I am searching for must not simply be expressed in the idioms of my culture, but seriously engage with and critique the culture. Since the culture that is emerging in Britain, and specifically in Northern Ireland, has never existed before we must work out the shape of the faithful life. Developing an adequate spirituality and defining the spiritual life is not something that can be done alone, it demands a community of people with the same foundational commitment and willingness to undertake the task of faithful improvisation. In summary, I feel like I am with Daniel in Babylon. I am looking for a group of friends who are determined to be faithful and to explore what that means in this time and place. The history and traditions of the community of faith will provide the resources from which to draw, but simply repeating the words and forms of previous years simply will not fit. The final shape of things is as yet unclear, and the journey toward settled forms will demand intense thought and debate within the community.

Studying the theme of exile has also helped me locate my ministry. I am a minister in a historic denomination, born within Christendom. According to the exile metaphor it is still in pre-exilic Jerusalem and shares many of the characteristics

---

86 J. Baker, D. Gay, and J. Brown, *Alternative Worship: Resources from and for the Emerging Church* (Baker Books, 2004), p xi.

and assumptions of that period explored in this paper. It is aware of threats coming from outside, and shares the same spectrum of responses. In my opinion the general response, however, is denial: denial that radical change is coming, denial that the church will be drastically weakened, denial that its influence in society will continue to be diminished, denial that God could be actively involved in this process, denial that the church could be systematically corrupt. There is an underlying assumption that since God has chosen the church as the instrument, sign and foretaste of the kingdom, such things ultimately can not happen. The process of writing this paper has convinced me that exile is the appropriate metaphor, and that we must therefore have a radical change of perspective. The problem is that, as in the time leading up to the exile, there is no way of being certain who is right, and I certainly do not claim to speak with the same authority as Jeremiah! Yet faithfulness demands that we act in accordance with what we have become convinced of, while having consideration for others.[87] Faithfulness is, therefore, risky, demanding personal commitment and sometimes action that is not in conformity with others. When the church is facing a crisis, such as it is, each of us is must become convinced of the correct interpretation and course of action, knowing that there will be no certainty as to who is right until much later. We also know that, within God's grace, faithfulness is what he prizes above being proved right, for 'they will stand, for the Lord is able to make them stand.'[88]

Applying the exile metaphor, and seeing that as denominations we are still in the pre-exile stage, I believe, also

---

87 See Rom 14.
88 Rom 14:4.

gives insight into the experience of many currently in ministry. There is a silent epidemic of stress related illness and people leaving ministry. The exile perspective suggests two possible reasons for this. First, that ministers and/or congregations may be working with the wrong metaphors for church. They may be working with a Christendom model that reflects the pre-exilic temple period, and be assuming that this model must continue. If this is the case, then increasing amounts of effort will be expended by fewer and fewer people to maintain things as they are. A slightly more subtle danger may come when decline is recognised and changes are proposed, but the underlying understanding and expectations of church remain unchanged. In this situation there will be initiatives to innovate with the expectation of restoring or reviving the church to its former glory. These initiatives will demand imagination and effort, but if exile is truly coming they will end with disappointment and disillusionment. Exile ultimately demands a paradigm shift in the model of church, not superficial changes. The second possible reason for stress in the ministry is among those who, explicitly or tacitly, recognise the radical nature of change that exile will bring to the church. Recognising this, they seek to explore and develop the new models that will be necessary. This is pioneering and demanding work, and thankfully there is an increasing community of people involved in a variety of expressions of it. Extra stress is created for those who are, at the same time, working within a congregation or denomination still operating with a Christendom model of church. They face the burden of seeking to keep the existing structures going in the meantime, to help their people prepare for exile and to begin to explore the models that will be relevant for the future.

This study has helped me to locate myself and my ministry. Personally I identify with Daniel, struggling to express the faithful life in the context in which I am living. I am minister of a congregation, and in a denomination, which is still largely 'pre-exilic' in its mindset. Brueggemann is correct in saying that my pastoral duty is to prepare the people for exile. This will be a long and difficult process, both for me and for those in my community. Giving up dearly held hopes and aspirations is not easy, especially when they are connected with our understandings of God and his faithfulness. Preparing the people for exile will mean sowing the seeds of a conception of church that does not assume buildings, staff and influence within society. It will mean helping people get used to the fact that living a faithful life no longer merely means living a decent life as defined by the surrounding society, for the community of faith and society no longer share the same basic assumptions. It will mean teaching people how to live a life of faithful improvisation, which will not simply repeat answers to questions of a previous era, but will seriously engage with issues as they are currently expressed and will look for a faithful response. It will mean being aware of the possibility of institutional blindness, and even syncretism, in our church life. It will mean re-learning a model of mission based on Christ saying 'As the Father has sent me, I am sending you';[89] a model that that does not rely on resources or influence. And it will mean constantly reminding people of hope in the midst of difficult circumstances. Just as the apocalyptic writers sought to show their struggling communities the reality lying behind the seemingly overwhelming power of the empire, so church communities

---

89 John 20:21.

facing great uncertainty and change must be reminded that God is still in control and faithful to his people.

When Lesslie Newbigin was bishop of Madras he used to be asked by visitors, 'Are you optimistic or pessimistic about the future of the church in India?' His standard reply was, 'I believe that Jesus rose from the dead, and therefore the question doesn't arise.' His point was, 'that in regard to a fact one is not optimistic or pessimistic. One is believing or unbelieving.'[90] Exile is a challenging experience at many levels. In the face of it our call is not to put on a brave face of optimism, but to explore and live the faithful life.

---

90 Newbigin, *A Word in Season - Perspectives on Christian World Missions*, p 55–6.

Bibliography

Allen, Roland. *Missionary Methods - St Paul's or Ours?* Grand Rapids, Michigan: Eerdmans, 1968.

Baker, J., D. Gay, and J. Brown. *Alternative Worship: Resources from and for the Emerging Church*. Baker Books, 2004.

Bayes, P., T. Sledge, and J. Holbrook. *Mission-Shaped Parish: Traditional Church in a Changing Context*. London: Church House Publishing, 2006.

Brown, Andrew. 'Why the Cornish Hotel Ruling Should Worry Conservative Christians'. *Guardian.co.uk*, May 11, 2011. http://www.guardian.co.uk/commentisfree/andrewbrown/2011/jan/18/cornish-hotel-ruling-conservative-christians.

Brueggemann, Walter. *Hopeful Imagination: Prophetic Voices in Exile*. Philadelphia: Fortress Press, 1986.

Brueggemann, Walter, and Patrick D Miller. *A Social Reading of the Old Testament - Prophetic Approaches to Israel's Communal Life*. Minneapolis: Fortress Press, 1994.

Brueggemann, Walter. *Theology of the Old Testament: Testimony, Dispute, Advocacy*. Minneapolis: Fortress Press, 2005.

'Changing Church for a Changing World | Fresh Expressions'. *Fresh Expressions*, February 13, 2012. http://www.freshexpressions.org.uk/.

Claiborne, S. *The Irresistible Revolution: Living as an Ordinary Radical*. Zondervan, 2008.

Council for World Mission. 'CWM Theology Statement 2010'. *CWM: A Partnership of Churches in Mission*, May 23, 2011. http://www.cwmission.org/theological-papers/cwm-theology-statement-2010.

Croft, E. S, and S. J.L Croft. *Mission Shaped Questions: Defining Issues for Today's Church*. London: Church House Publishing, 2008.

Freeman, Andy. *Punk Monk*. Eastbourne: Survivor, 2004.

Gaze, S. *Mission-Shaped and Rural: Growing Churches in the Countryside*. London: Church House Publishing, 2006.

Harper, I. R. L, and Samuel Gregg. *Christian Theology and Market Economics*. Cheltenham: Edward Elgar, 2008.

Hope, S. *Mission-Shaped Spirituality: The Transforming Power of Mission*. London: Church House Publishing, 2006.

Hull, J. *Mission-Shaped Church: A Theological Response*. London: SCM Press, 2006.

Küng, Hans. *Theology for the Third Millennium: An Ecumenical View*. London: Harper Collins, 1991.

Mobsby, I. J. *Emerging and Fresh Expressions of Church: How Are They Authentically Church and Anglican?* London: Moot Community Publishing, 2008.

Newbigin, Lesslie. *A Word in Season - Perspectives on Christian World Missions*. Grand Rapids, Michigan: Eerdmans, 1994.

———. *Foolishness to the Greeks - the Gospel and Western Culture*. London: SPCK, 1986.

———. *The Gospel in a Pluralist Society*. Grand Rapids, Michigan: Eerdmans, 1989.

———. *The Household of God*. London: SCM Press, 1951.

———. *The Open Secret - An Introduction to the Theology of Mission*. Grand Rapids, Michigan: Eerdmans, 1995.

Northumbria Community, and Northumbria Community Staff. *Celtic Daily Prayer*. London: Harper Collins, 2005.

Peskett, Howard, and Vinoth Ramachandra. *The Message of Mission - The Glory of Christ In All Time and Space*. Leicester: Inter-Varsity Press, 2003.

Ramachandra, Vinoth. *Gods That Fail: Modern Idolatry and Christian Mission.* Carlisle, Cumbria: Paternoster Press, 1996.

Stevenson, J. *A New Eusebius: Documents Illustrating the History of the Church to AD 337.* SPCK, 1995.

The Northumbria Community. 'Building the New on Foundations of Old'. *The Northumbria Community,* June 22, 2011. http://www.northumbriacommunity.org/sharing-wisdom/347-building-the-new-on-foundations-of-old?showall=1.

———. 'Who Are We? Well, Let's Begin Here...' *The Northumbria Community,* June 22, 2011. http://www.northumbriacommunity.org/who-we-are.

Thomas F Foust, George R Hunsberger, J. Andrew Kirk, and Werner Ustorf. *A Scandalous Prophet - the Way of Mission After Newbigin.* Edited by Thomas F Foust, George R Hunsberger, J. Andrew Kirk, and Werner Ustorf. Grand Rapids, Michigan: Eerdmans, 2002.

University of Exeter. 'The Change Curve', June 27, 2011. http://www.exeter.ac.uk/media/universityofexeter/humanresources/documents/learningdevelopment/the_change_curve.pdf.

Walsh, B. J, and S. C Keesmaat. *Colossians Remixed: Subverting the Empire.* Milton Keynes: Paternoster, 2005.

Withers, Margaret. *Mission-Shaped Children: Moving Towards a Child-Centred Church.* London: Church House Publishing, 2006.

Working Group of Church of England's Mission and Public Affairs Council. *Mission-shaped Church - Church Planting and Fresh Expressions of Church in a*

Changing Context. London: Church House Publishing, 2004.

Wright, N. T. *The New Testament and the People of God.* Fortress Press, 1996.

About Contemporary Christianity

Over the last 25 years Evangelical Contribution on Northern Ireland (ECONI) and its successors, the Centre for Contemporary Christianity in Ireland (2005-2010) and Contemporary Christianity (since 2010), have encouraged the Christian community in Northern Ireland to think biblically about its peace-building vocation. ECONI emerged against the backdrop of the stark community division and political violence in Northern Ireland, with a group of evangelical Christians arguing for a new response. Their conviction was that faithful witness must take seriously the biblical command to make peace and do justice. Where loyalty to political and cultural identities had obscured loyalty to Jesus Christ, Christians needed to rediscover what it means to live for God and His Gory Alone. We have always sought to look honestly at our own community, leading us to ask tough questions and acknowledge sectarian attitudes and practices. In Christ we believe God is reconciling the world and so we must continually seek realistic ways to deal with historical divisions and heal the wounds of the past. But while the challenges of building a peaceful and inclusive society continue locally, there are bigger challenges now facing us in the form of wider changes in society.

How do the people of God remain faithful to the vision of the Kingdom, when greed, evil and injustice seem to rule, when there is more heartache than happiness in being citizens set in time and space, in fallen cities and nations? Something is better than nothing. We can make peace with some justice, some mercy, continually remembering that it will only be in the new heaven and new earth that we will see all of the conditions for human flourishing finally in place, socially, economically, and politically. In Contemporary Christianity we believe that, in a small way, we can make a difference here and now in helping the church to be good news. There are no quick fixes or easy answers and we are committed to take risks that will involve stretching our faith, knowing that there is nothing in our world outside the scope of God's grace and love.

Noel McCune

Chairperson
Contemporary Christianity
www.contemporarychristianity.net
August 2012